Trace Lines

To Parents: In this activity, your child will practice drawing sh[...] vertical lines. When your child is ready to trace with crayons, ha[...] them use crayons that are easy to color with. Children of this a[...] usually do not apply much pressure when writing.

  Trace lines from to . Put a sticker on .

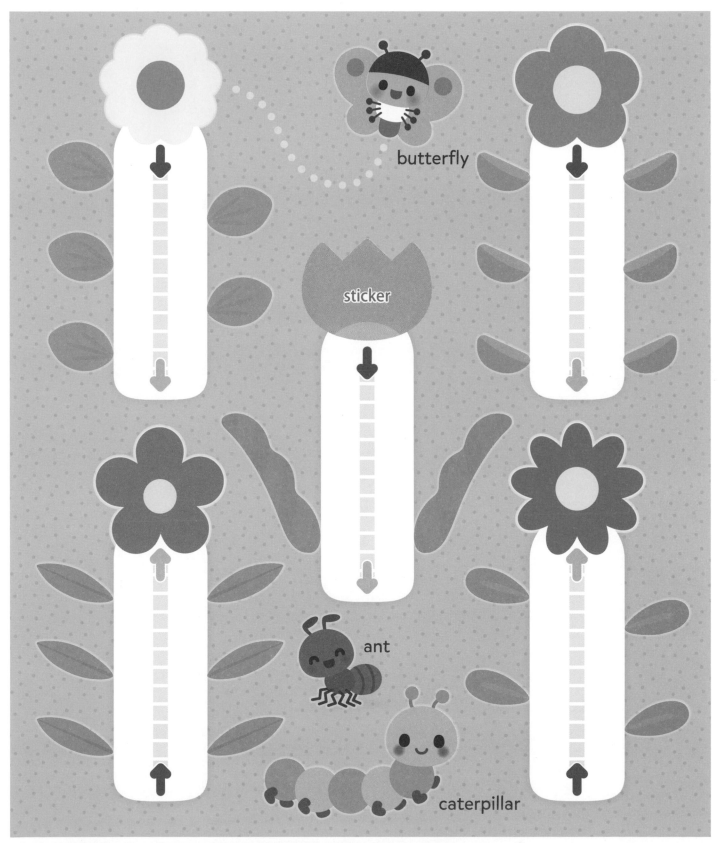

butterfly

sticker

ant

caterpillar

Bonus Challenge! Point to each insect and say its name.

Sticker

Good job!

Trace Lines

To Parents: In this activity, your child will practice drawing diagonal lines. It's okay if your child draws a line longer than the dotted lines. When they're finished, praise your child, saying, "Well done!"

Trace lines from ➡ to ➡.

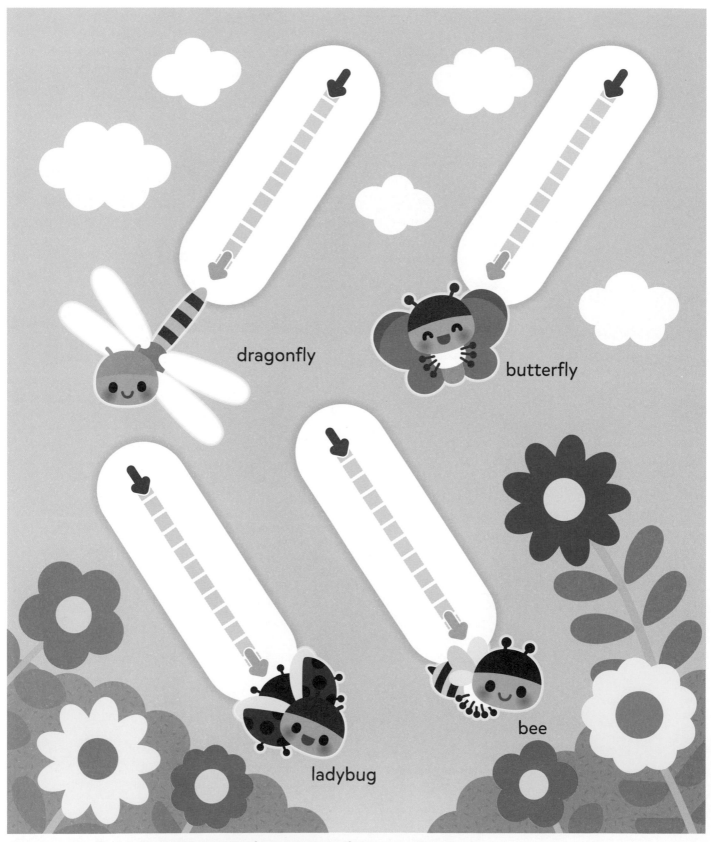

dragonfly

butterfly

ladybug

bee

Bonus Challenge! Point to each insect and say its name.

Trace Lines

To Parents: In this activity, your child will practice drawing short horizontal lines. Tell them to help the animal parent meet the child.

Sticker
Good job!

  Trace lines from to . Put the stickers on .

giraffe

elephant

sticker

sticker

lion

hippo

Bonus Challenge! Point to each animal and say its name.

4

Trace Lines

To Parents: In this activity, your child will practice drawing wavy lines and zigzags. If that seems difficult, encourage your child first to slowly trace the lines with their finger.

Trace lines from ➡ to ➡.

ship

sailboat

train

bus

Bonus Challenge! Point to each vehicle and say its name.

Trace Lines

To Parents: In this activity, your child will practice drawing short curved lines and ovals. If this seems difficult, put your hand on your child's to help them draw. It's okay if they don't trace well.

 Trace lines from ➡ to ➡.

balloon

airplane

helicopter

UFO

Bonus Challenge! Point to each vehicle and say its name.

Trace the Moon

To Parents: In this activity, your child will practice drawing a continuous line. Encourage them to pause at each corner before continuing.

  Trace line from to . Put the ☆ stickers in the night sky.

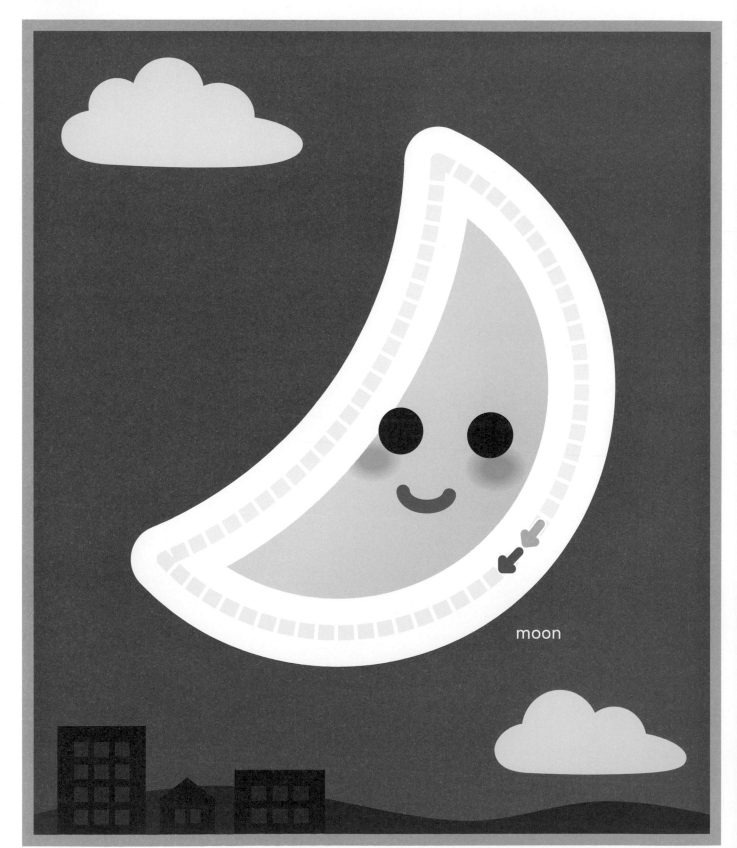

moon

Trace the Sun

To Parents: This activity is designed to teach your child how to draw a circle and diagonal lines. It is difficult to draw a circle, so encourage them to take a rest after drawing a semicircle.

 Trace lines from ➡ to ➡.

sun

Bonus Challenge! Count the number of birds.

8

Trace the Bear's Face

  Trace line from to . Put a sticker on .

sticker

bear

Trace the Dog's Face

To Parents: Your child may have difficulty tracing a continuous line without resting. Encourage them to pause at each corner.

Sticker

Good job!

  Trace line from to . Put a sticker on ⬤.

sticker

dog

Find the Path to the Toy Box

To Parents: First, ask your child, "Where should you put your toys?" Then, tell them to trace only one of the two lines.

 Put the toys away. Which dotted line leads to the toy box?
Trace the line from ➡ to ➡.

toys

TOYS

Find the Path to the Bookshelf

To Parents: First, ask your child, "Where should you put your books?" Encourage them to trace each dotted line with their finger to find the correct path before tracing it with a crayon.

 Put the books away. Which dotted line leads to the bookshelf? Trace the line from ➡ to ➡.

books

Find the Path to the Bear Cubs

To Parents: In this activity, the dotted lines cross in complex ways. Tell your child that they can move forward even where the lines overlap.

Help the mother bear get to her cubs. Which dotted line leads to the bear cubs? Trace the line from ➡ to ➡.

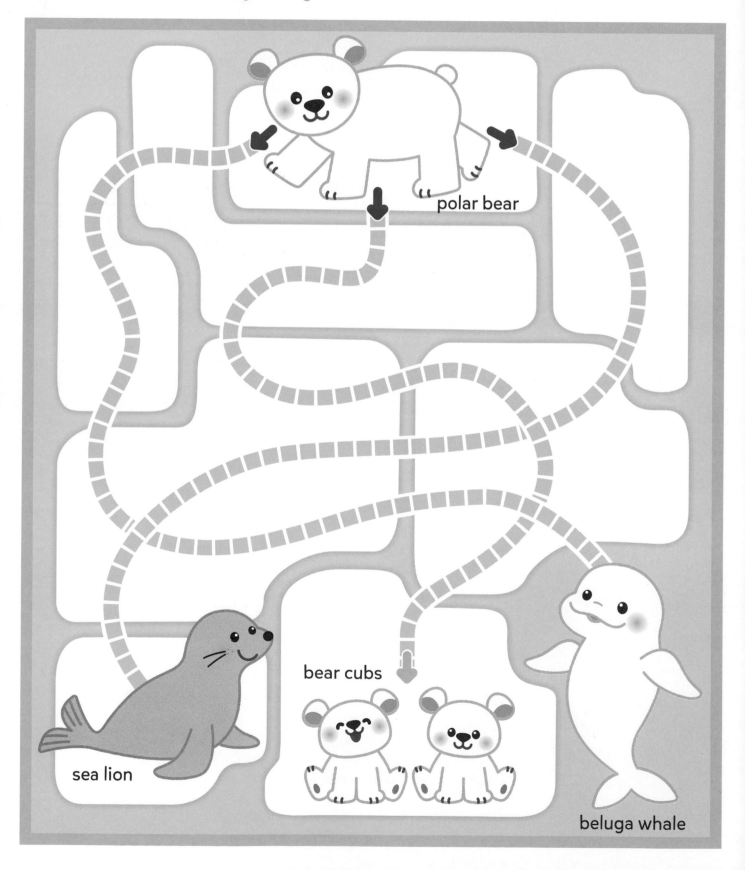

polar bear

sea lion

bear cubs

beluga whale

Find the Path to the Beehive

To Parents: Ask your child, "Which path leads to the beehive?" Encourage them to follow each path with their finger before using a crayon to trace the correct path.

 Help the bee get to the beehive. Which dotted line leads to the beehive? Trace the line from ➡ to ➡.

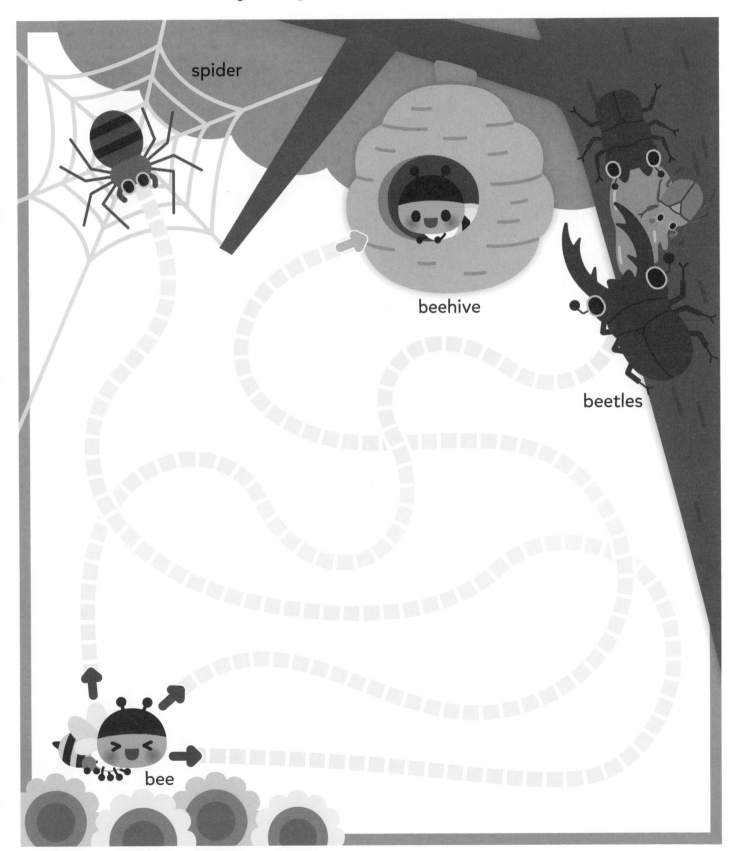

Draw a Line

To Parents: In this activity, the dotted line gets your child started. Encourage them to draw a line that keeps the remote control truck on the white path.

Drive your remote control truck on the path. Draw a line from ➡ to ➡.

Bonus Challenge! Count the number of houses with chimneys.

Draw a Line

To Parents: The shape in this activity is made up of different types of lines (curved and horizontal). When turning a corner, have your child stop the crayon momentarily before continuing.

 Take a ride on the skateboard. Draw a line from to ➡.

Match What You Use

To Parents: Start the activity by asking, "What do you use when you wash your hands/brush your teeth?" Then, have your child connect each activity with the correct items.

Which of these items do you use when you wash your hands? Which of these items do you use when you brush your teeth? Draw each line from ➡ to ➡.

toothpaste

cup

soap

towel

Go to the Bathroom

To Parents: Before your child starts the activity, say to them, "The girl wants to go to the bathroom. How can she get to the bathroom? Let's take her there!"

 Take the girl to the bathroom. Draw a line from ➡ to ➡.

Go Through the Maze

To Parents: This activity prompts children to draw a line within the white area. Since there isn't a guide, it's okay if the line isn't smooth.

 Take the lamb to the mother sheep. Draw a line from ➡ to ➡. Then, make the animals' noises.

Bonus Challenge! Point to each animal and say its name.

Feed the Cows

To Parents: Your child may put the grass stickers on before drawing their line, or they may draw the line first. Let them choose the way they want to do it.

Good job!

   Draw a line from ➡ to ➡ while giving each cow a grass sticker. Then, make the animals' noises.

Bonus Challenge! Point to each animal and say its name.

Fold the Panda

To Parents: This is a maze with a forked path. If your child goes the wrong way, encourage them to go back to the forked path and start again.

Fold →

How to Play

Draw a line from ➡ to ➡. Then, fold along the - - - and —·— lines for a surprise!

Fold down

Fold up

Find the Surprise

To Parents: Before folding the page, ask your child, "What is hidden in this picture?"

Sticker

Good job!

  Draw a line from ➡ to ➡. Then, fold along the – – – and —·— lines for a surprise!

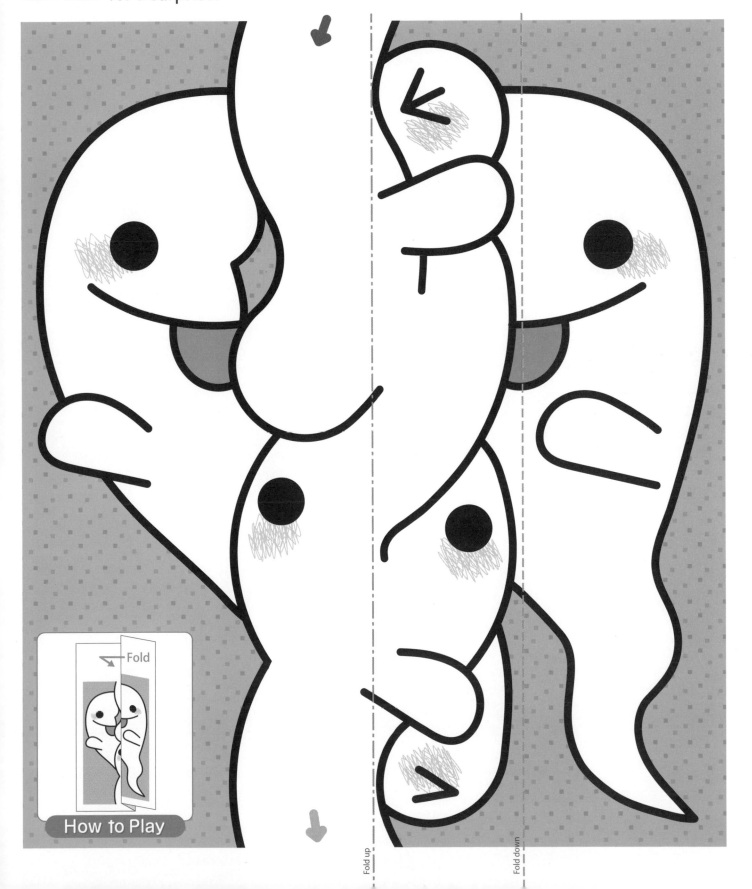

Fold

How to Play

Fold up

Fold down

Go Through the Maze

To Parents: In this activity, your child will practice drawing a line without using a guide. Tell them to stop drawing when they need to change direction, then start again.

Get the zebra back to the herd. Draw a line from ➡ to ➡.

zebra

Find the Fishbowl

To Parents: In this activity, your child will practice drawing a continuous line. Encourage them to draw the path without lifting their pencil or crayon.

 Put the goldfish in the fishbowl. Draw a line from ➡ to ➡.

goldfish

Go Through the Tree

To Parents: Encourage your child to study the entire picture and to think carefully before deciding which path to take.

Draw a line from ➡ to ➡.

Bonus Challenge! Say the name of each animal that lives in the tree.

Go Through the Sea

To Parents: After drawing a line from the clown fish to the turtle, encourage your child to stop momentarily before continuing their line to the jellyfish. This will help them draw a longer line.

Sticker

Good job!

 Draw a line from ➡ to ➡.

clown fish

turtle

jellyfish

crab

shrimp

squid

octopus

Bonus Challenge! Say the name of each creature that lives in the sea.

Follow the Cupcakes

To Parents: This activity is designed to help your child recognize objects that are the same. Encourage your child to trace the path with their finger first, then let them do it with a crayon.

Follow the cupcakes to get from ➡ to ➡.

juice

cupcake

donut

cookie

Bonus Challenge! Count the number of cupcakes.

Follow the Fire Trucks

To Parents: This activity also focuses on recognizing similar objects. Ask your child, "Where can you find each vehicle?"

Follow the fire trucks to get from ➡ to ➡.

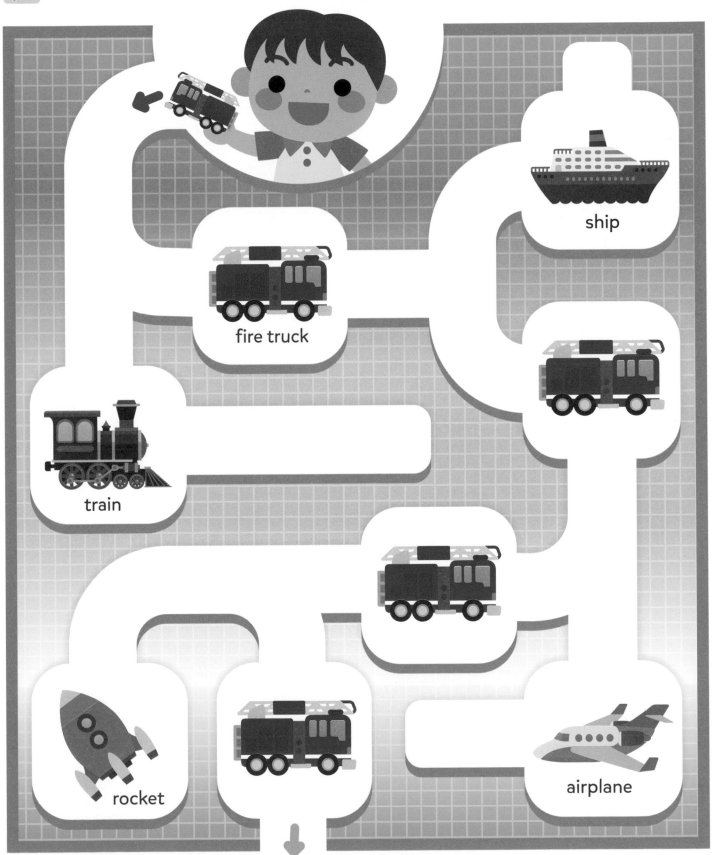

ship

fire truck

train

rocket

airplane

Bonus Challenge! Count the number of fire trucks.

Follow the Numbers in Order

To Parents: This activity focuses on number sequence. Have your child follow the path of numbers in order from 1 to 3. Say the numbers out loud as you go.

 Draw a line from ➡ to ➡, following the path from 1 → 2 → 3.

Bonus Challenge! Count the number of flowers.

Follow the ABCs in Order

To Parents: Draw a line while saying A, B, C, D. When your child has finished drawing the line and coloring, say, "A is for apple, B is for balloon, C is for corn, D is for dolphin."

  Draw a line from ➡ to ➡, following the path from A → B → C → D. When finished, color the apple, balloon, corn, and dolphin.

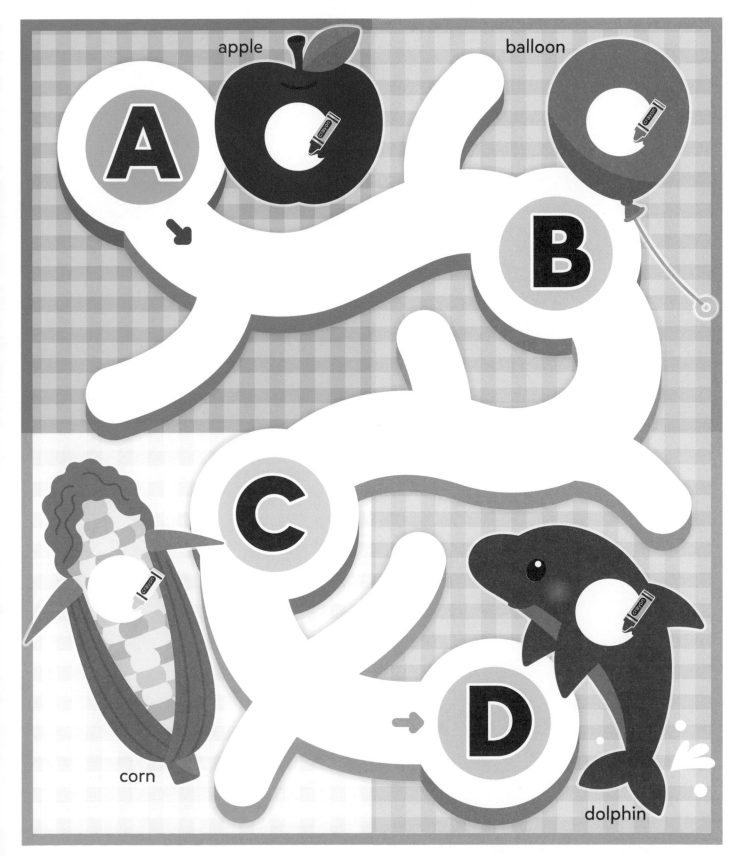

apple

balloon

corn

dolphin

Match Socks

To Parents: Before starting, tell your child that the same socks should be together. This will help them develop a sense of organization.

Draw lines from ➡ to ➡ to match the two socks.

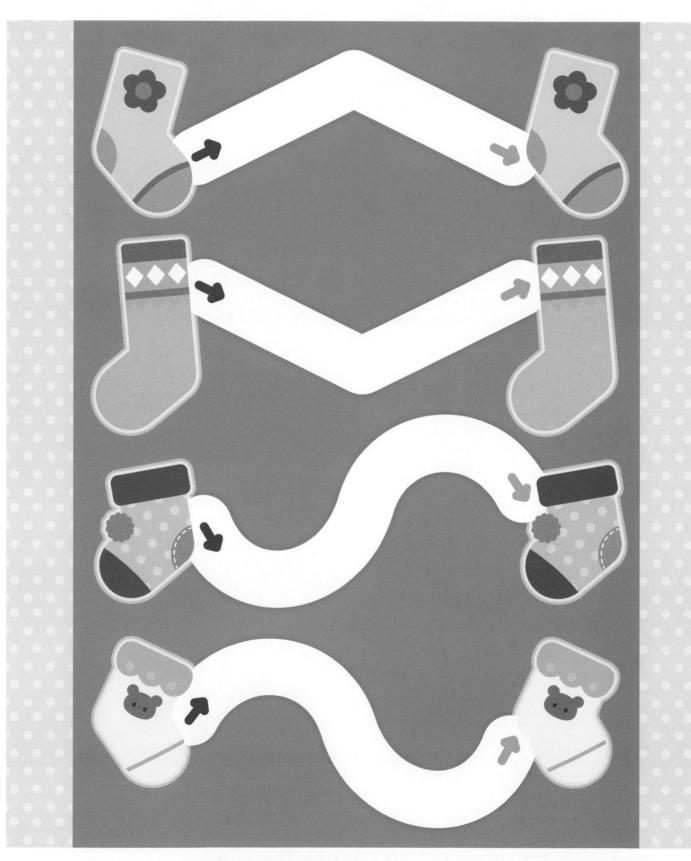

Match Gloves

To Parents: Tell your child that gloves are used together. Ask them, "When will you use gloves?"

 Draw lines from ➡ to ➡ to match the two gloves.

Good job! Sticker

Draw Lines

To Parents: It is difficult to draw a spiral line. Encourage your child first to trace each shape with their finger so they can learn the shape and direction of each line before using a crayon or pencil.

 Draw lines from ➡ to ➡. Put the stickers on   .

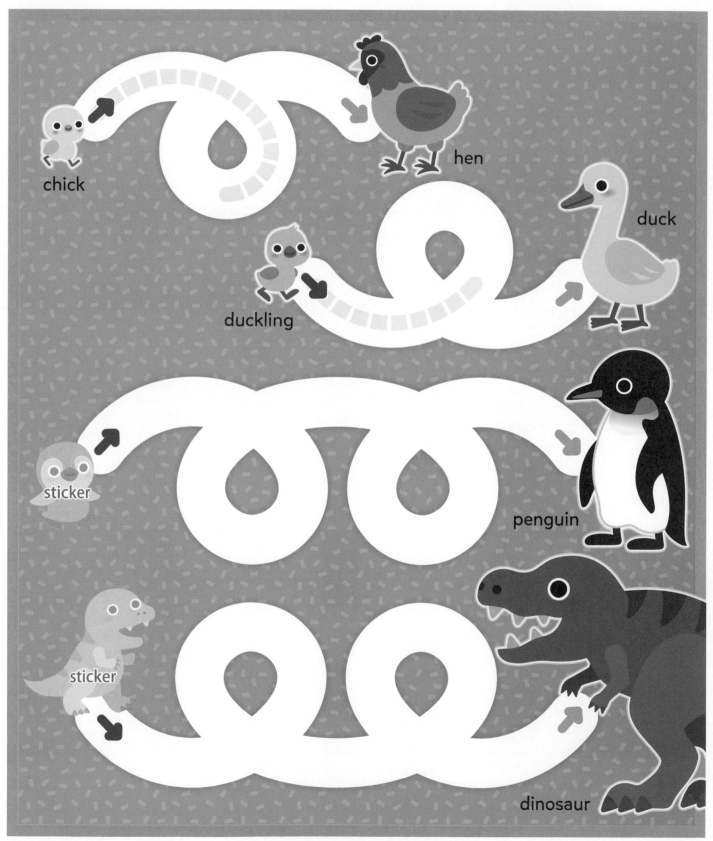

chick

hen

duck

duckling

sticker

penguin

sticker

dinosaur

Bonus Challenge! Point to each animal and say its name.

Draw Lines

To Parents: This activity focuses on drawing consecutive horizontal zigzags and arches. Make sure your child stops at the end of each arc and bend before moving on to the next.

  Draw lines from ➡ to ➡. Put the stickers on .

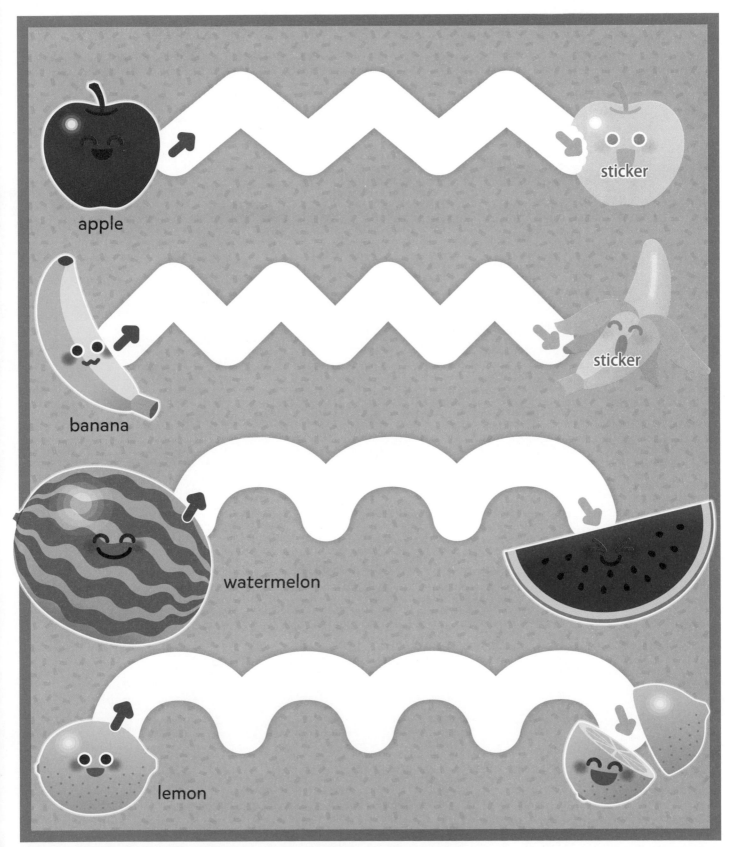

apple

sticker

banana

sticker

watermelon

lemon

Bonus Challenge! Point to each fruit and say its name.

Sticker
★ Good job! ★

Follow the Paths

To Parents: This activity focuses on drawing consecutive vertical zigzags and arches. Ask your child, "What do you use for eating ice cream? What do you use for eating pasta?"

 Draw lines from ➡ to ➡.

Draw Spirals

To Parents: In this activity, your child will practice drawing right- and left-turning spirals. Make sure your child pays attention to the direction of the pink and blue arrows.

 Draw lines from ➡ to ➡.

Bonus Challenge! Count the number of green fish.

Sticker

Good job!

Trace the Animals' Faces

To Parents: After your child traces the lines, say, "The pig's face is a circle, and the cow's face is a square." This will help them remember the shapes.

Trace lines from ➡ to ➡. Say the name of each shape.

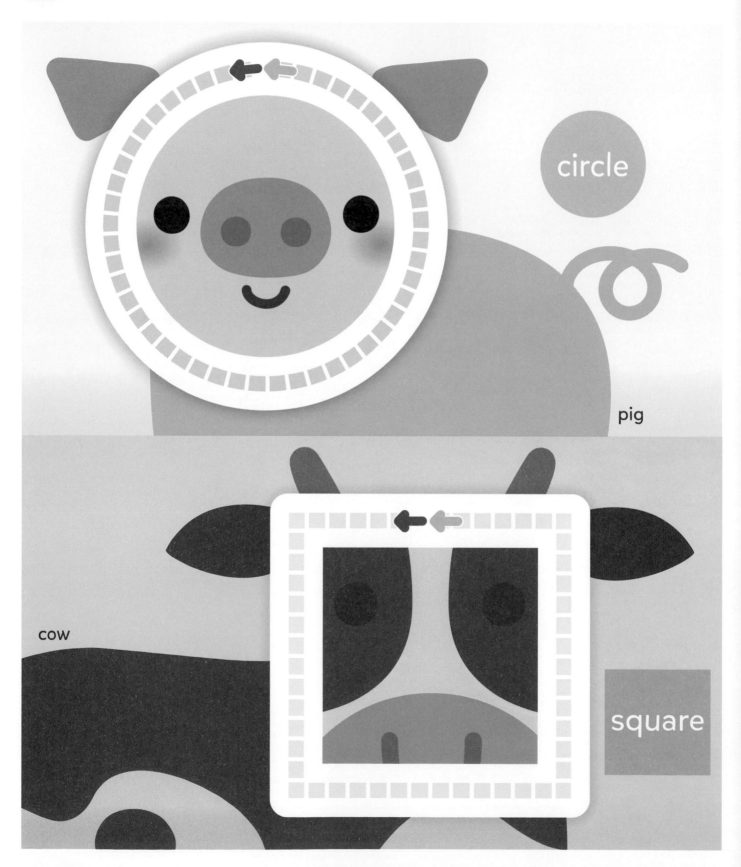

circle

pig

cow

square

Trace the Animals' Faces

To Parents: After your child traces the lines, say, "The fox's face is a triangle, and the mouse's face is a heart."

 Trace lines from ➡ to ➡. Say the name of each shape.

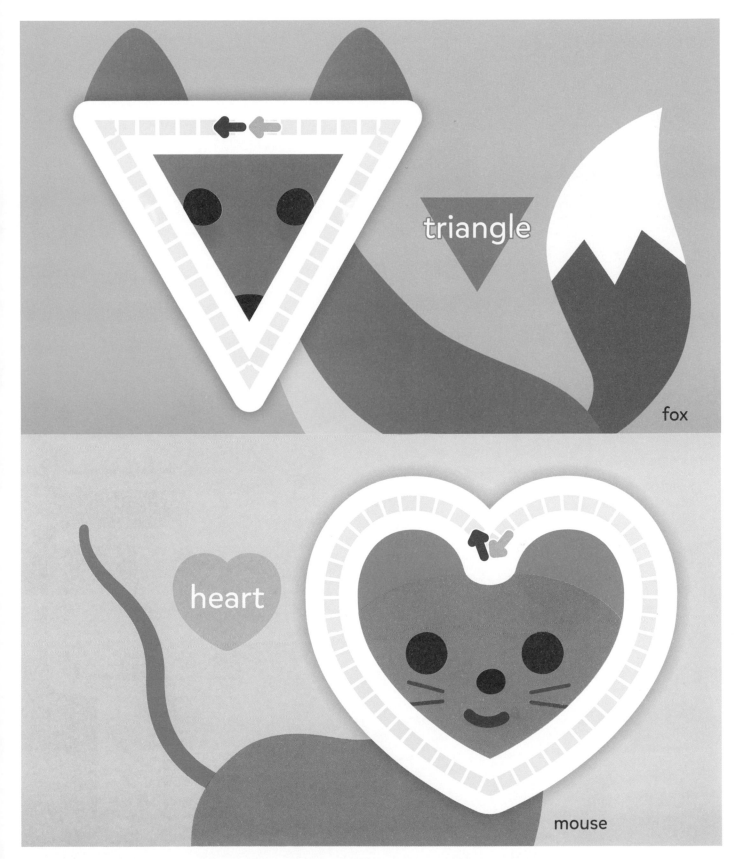

triangle

fox

heart

mouse

Follow the Path with More Things

To Parents: In this activity, your child will count and compare quantities. They may count to see which way the path should go, but if possible, have them practice judging the amount by appearance without counting.

 Draw a line from ➡ to ➡, following the path that has more objects.

Follow the Path with Bigger Things

To Parents: Before beginning this activity, compare your hand and shoe size with your child's so they can see the difference between large and small.

 Draw a line from ➡ to ➡, following the path that has the larger object.

Follow the Path Through the Dinosaur

To Parents: This is a maze where the width of the path changes. If it is difficult for your child, encourage them to go toward the nearest narrow path! Following the narrow paths leads your child to the exit.

Draw a line from ➡ to ➡ through the dinosaur.

Follow the Path Through the Turtle

To Parents: Have your child draw a path through the turtle maze without crossing over any lines.

Sticker
Good job!

 Draw a line from ➡ to ➡ through the turtle.

Follow the Path Through the Grapes

To Parents: Encourage your child to draw carefully to avoid hitting the sides of the path. Completing mazes helps build fine motor control.

 Draw a line from ➡ to ➡ through the grapes.

Follow the Path Through the Pumpkin

To Parents: Completing mazes also helps develop handwriting skills and the ability to look ahead before making a decision. Encourage your child to try again from the beginning if they hit a dead end.

Draw a line from ➡ to ➡ through the pumpkin.

Fold down   Fold down

44

Follow the Path to the Rabbit

44

To Parents: First, look at the two bushes at the bottom, then ask your child, "Where is the rabbit hiding?" Encourage your child to trace the two paths with their finger first to make sure they are following the right one before drawing their line. When they reach the end, open the flap to reveal the rabbit!

 Which path leads to the hidden rabbit? Draw a line from ➡ to ➡ and open the bushes to find the rabbit.

Fold up

Fold up

Fold

How to Play

Follow the Path to the Mole

To Parents: Encourage your child to pay attention to the entire picture and think carefully before deciding which path to take.

Which path leads to the mole? Draw a line from ➡ to ➡ and open the holes to find the mole.

How to Play

Get Dressed

To Parents: In this activity, your child will learn the habit of getting dressed. Move to each piece of clothing, saying, "Put on a shirt, then put on pants..."

  Draw a line from ➡ to ➡ while putting shirt and shoe stickers on the path.

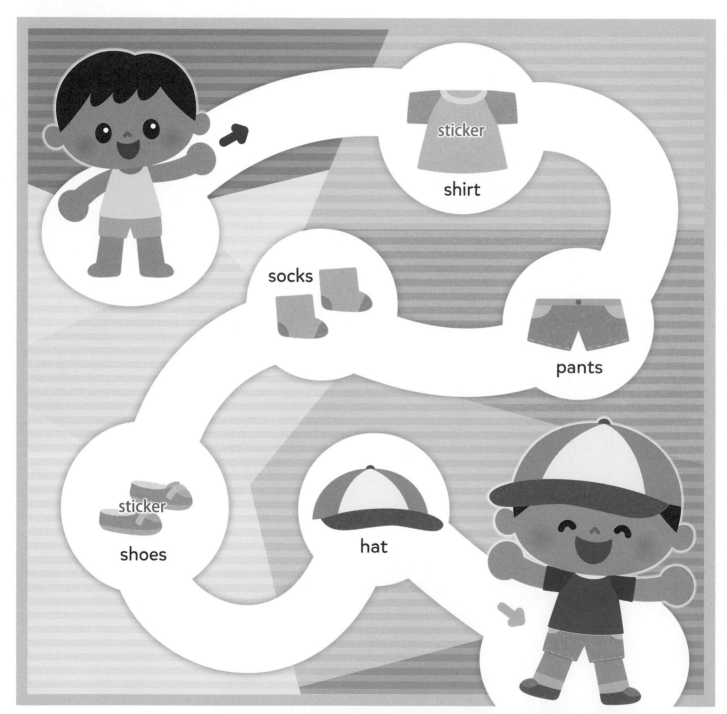

sticker
shirt

socks

pants

sticker
shoes

hat

Fold down   Fold down   Fold down

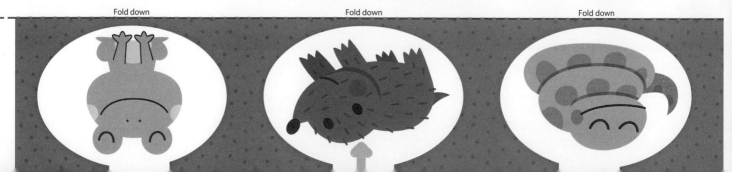

Gather Vegetables

To Parents: In this activity, your child will collect vegetables. As you pass each vegetable, say its name.

  Draw a line from ➡ to ➡ while putting tomato and eggplant stickers on the path.

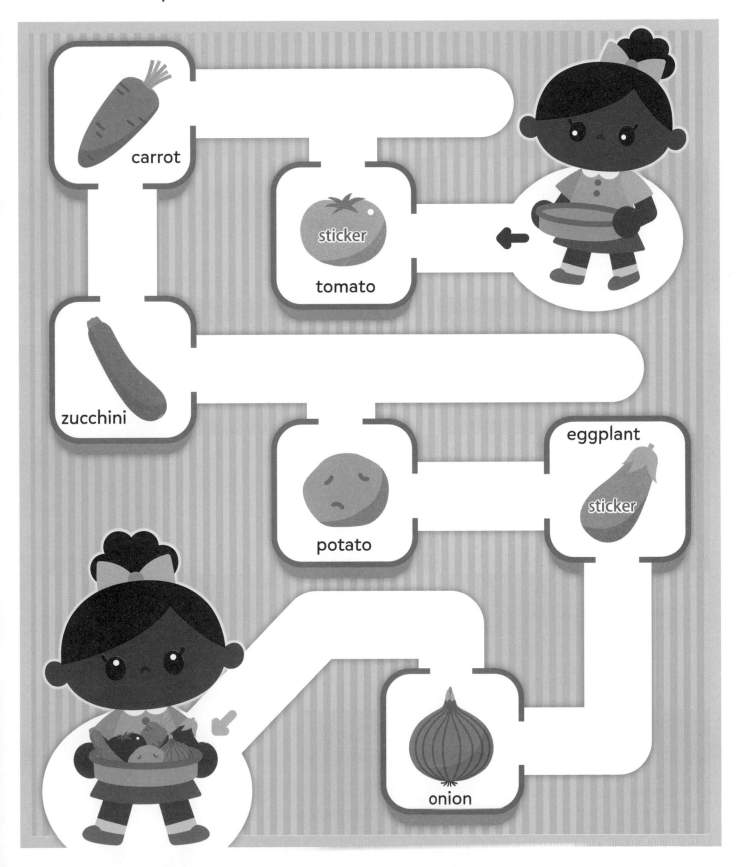

Sticker

Good job!

Go Through the Jungle

To Parents: At the junction on page 49, ask your child, "Which path should you take to get to safety?" Open the door of their choice and try again if they find a crocodile!

  Draw a line from ➡ to ➡ to get through the jungle. Which is the safer path on page 49? Once you choose a path, open the door.

parrot

spider

slot

toucan

leopard

butterfly

Bonus Challenge! Find blue butterflies on pages 48 and 49 and circle them.

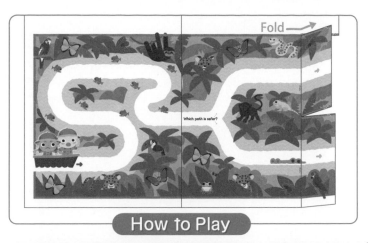

How to Play

snake

Fold up

hich path is safer?

monkey

iguana

frog

Fold up

Fold up

Fold up

Bonus Challenge! Say the name of each animal that lives in the jungle.

50

Go Through the Monster Maze

To Parents: Your child can draw a straight line or a curvy line. It will be fun to intentionally draw the line close to the monsters.

Draw a line from ➡ to ➡ without touching the monsters.

We did it!

It's a crocodile!

Go Through the Bird Maze

To Parents: Tell your child that if the line gets too close to the birds, the birds will pop the balloon. If the line touches the bird, imitate the sound of a balloon bursting.

Draw a line from ➡ to ➡ without touching the clouds or birds.

example

Bonus Challenge! Count the number of pink birds.

Follow the Crayon Maze

To Parents: Make sure your child understands that they should navigate the maze following the direction of the tips of the crayons.

 Draw a line from ➡ to ➡, following the direction the crayons are pointing.

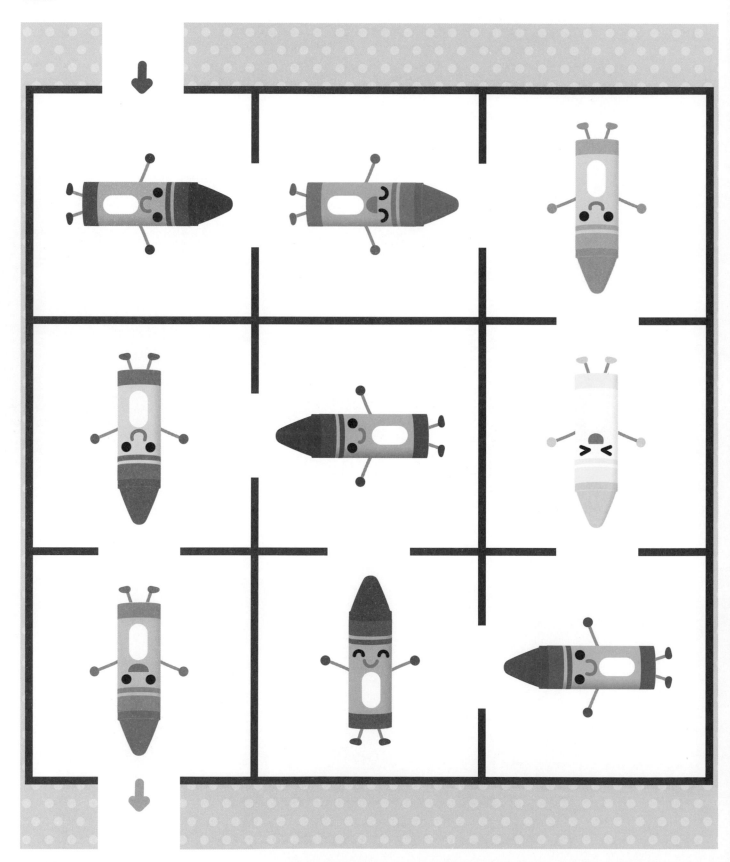

Follow the Cats' Eyes

To Parents: Make sure your child understands that they should navigate the maze following the direction of the cats' eyes.

 Draw a line from ➡ to ➡, following the direction of each cat's eyes.

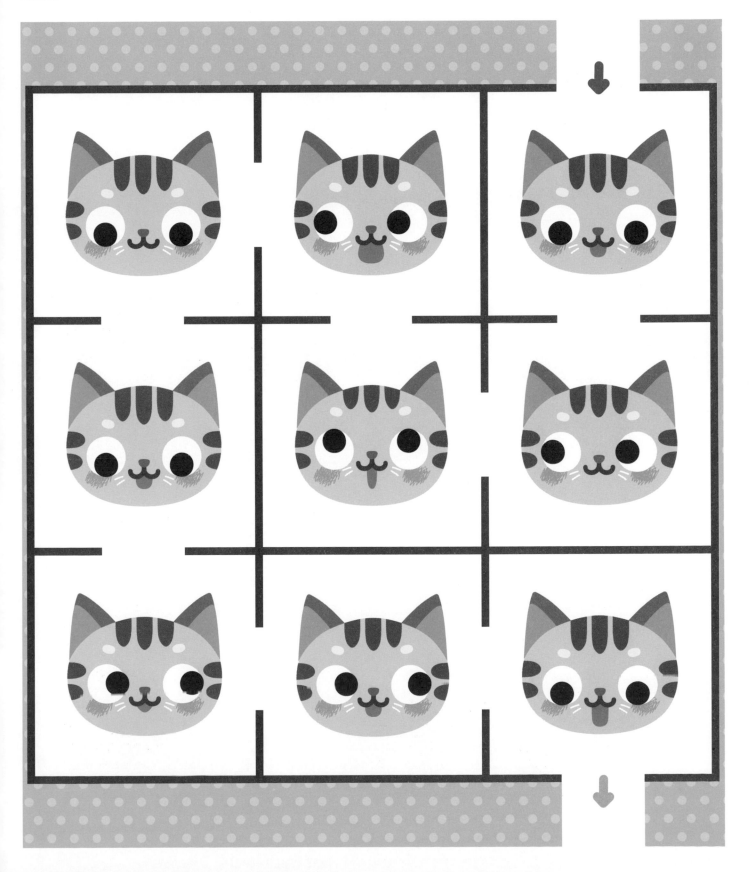

Follow the Cactus Path

To Parents: This activity is designed to help your child recognize objects that are the same. Tell them that they are the same cactus, even though they have different facial expressions.

Draw a line from ➡ to ➡ through the path with the cacti.

lizard

owl

hedgehog

snake

scorpion

Bonus Challenge! Say the name of each animal that lives in the desert.

Fix the Bridge

To Parents: First, let your child follow the path with their finger so they understand the path is not complete. Then, ask them, "The dog will fall into the ocean, won't it? How will the dog get to the dog house?" This will help them develop problem-solving skills.

  The bridge is broken. Put stickers on [sticker] to fix the bridge. Then, draw a line from ➡ to ➡.

Follow the Piglets

To Parents: First, have your child look at the picture at the top right of the page so they understand there is a mother pig and two baby piglets. Then, look at the picture of the mother pig at the bottom of the page and tell them to take her to her piglets.

Draw a line through the path with the piglets.

cat

piglet

wolf

pig

Go Through the Maze

To Parents: Tell your child, "There is a park behind the two kids, and the park will be cleaner if they properly throw away their garbage."

Sticker
Good job!

 Throw your garbage into the recycling bin. Draw a line from ➡ to ➡.

Sticker

Good job!

Follow the Red Things

To Parents: Follow the path to find objects that are the same color. Ask your child, "Which ones are blue? Which are yellow?"

crayon

 Draw a line through the path with the red objects.

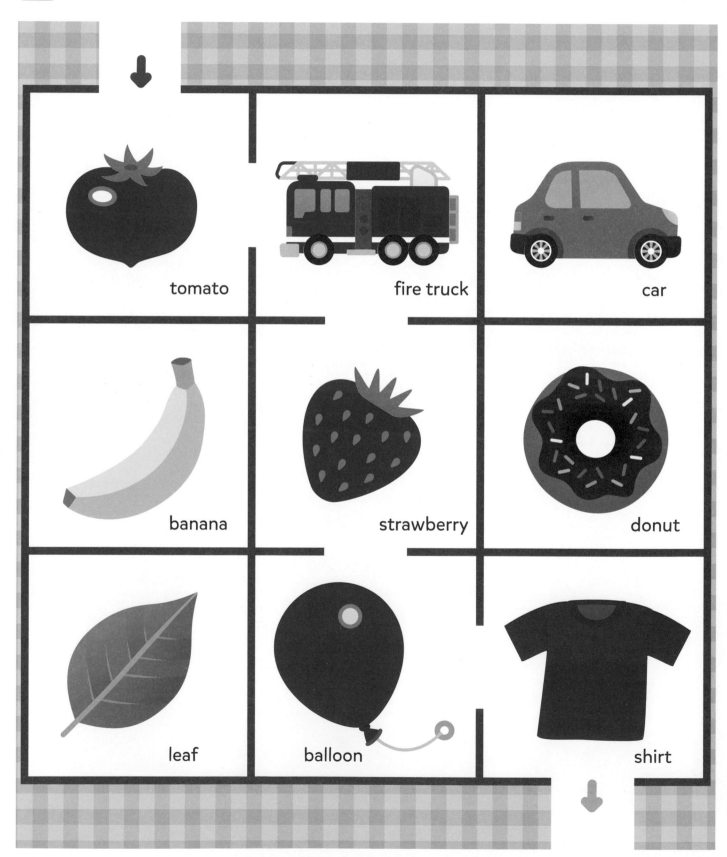

tomato

fire truck

car

banana

strawberry

donut

leaf

balloon

shirt

Follow the Pandas

To Parents: In this activity, your child will practice finding the same animal among other animals. Point to each animal and say its name.

Sticker

Good job!

 Draw a line through the path with the panda faces.

panda

lion

hippo

giraffe

elephant

Bonus Challenge! Count the number of pandas.

Make a Pattern

To Parents: In this activity, your child must recognize similarities in objects and then put those objects in order according to a pattern or sequence. Have your child say the name of each item out loud (star, heart, star, heart).

  Draw a line from to . Add stickers to complete the pattern.

Follow the Numbers in Order

To Parents: This activity is designed to teach number sequence. If your child is having a hard time, practice counting from 1 to 5 a few times and then have them try again.

 Draw a line from ➡ to ➡, following the path from 1 → 2 → 3 → 4 → 5. Say the numbers out loud as you go.

62

Sticker
★ Good job! ★

Follow the Numbers in Order

To Parents: First, encourage your child to practice counting from 1 to 7. Then, tell them to follow the path in numerical order.

Draw a line from → to →, following the path from l → 2 → 3 → 4 → 5 → 6 → 7. Say the numbers out loud as you go. Then, put the caterpillar sticker on .

Find All the Turtles

To Parents: Make sure your child visits every turtle in the maze without taking the same path twice. Let them know it is okay if they do not find the correct path on the first few tries.

Sticker
Good job!

 Baby turtles just hatched! Draw a line from ➡ to ➡ through the path with all five sea turtles without taking the same path twice.

Find All the Animals

To Parents: Have your child complete the maze without taking the same path twice. Be sure they visit all the animals.

Draw a line from 🐵 → 🐒 → 🐘 → 🐨 → 🐱 → 🐼 without taking the same path twice.

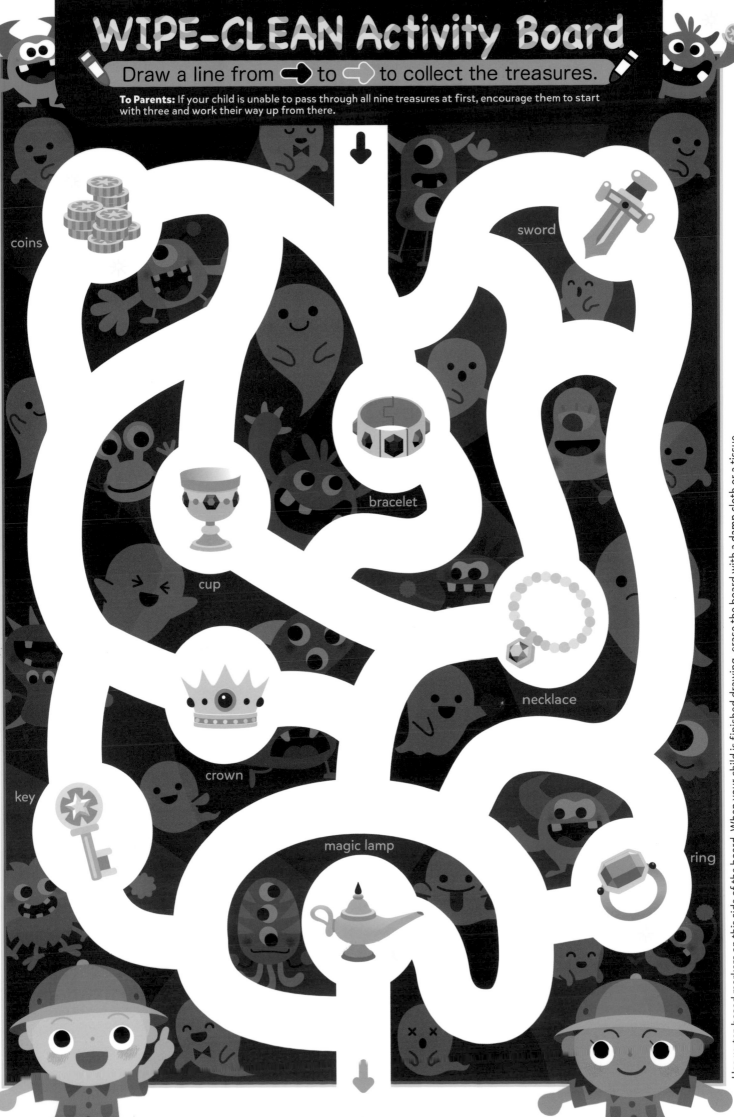

WIPE-CLEAN Activity Board

Draw a line from ⟹ to ⟸ to collect the treasures.

To Parents: If your child is unable to pass through all nine treasures at first, encourage them to start with three and work their way up from there.

coins

sword

bracelet

cup

necklace

crown

key

magic lamp

ring

Use water-based markers on this side of the board. When your child is finished drawing, erase the board with a damp cloth or a tissue.

Find the animals, vegetables, and vehicles. Circle each group in a different color. Finally, find the garbage.

To Parents: In this activity, your child will practice sorting things by group. Circle each group in a different color. Then, ask them where they put their garbage.

cow

pumpkin

plastic bottle

ship

cat

corn

airplane

plastic bag

potato

dog

train

pig

used paper

onion

empty can

car

animals: cow/cat/dog/pig **vegetables:** pumpkin/corn/potato/onion **vehicles:** ship/airplane/train/car **garbage:** plastic bottle/plastic bag/used paper/empty can